THE
BEAVER POND

by Alvin Tresselt

ILLUSTRATED BY
Roger Duvoisin

LOTHROP, LEE & SHEPARD COMPANY, NEW YORK

The beavers had made the pond in the first place.
Here in a hidden valley, where a small stream
wandered through a grove of aspen trees,
the beavers built a dam.
With their sharp teeth they cut down young aspen trees
to eat the bark. Then they dragged the trunks
and branches to the brook for the dam.
They criss-crossed the sticks just so,
and plastered them over with mud and stones
to hold back the rushing water of the stream.

Larger and larger the pond grew, and in the middle
of the still water the beavers built their domed houses,

with tunnels under the water, so no enemies could get in.
In time green reeds sprang up along the shore.

They waved their pointy fingers in the breeze,
and redwinged blackbirds came to hide their nests
in the rustly grasses.
Ducks came, too, for the beaver pond was a good place
for ducklings to swim and dive.
Fish swam down the stream into the pond,
and a blue kingfisher perched on a limb
to watch for fish for his dinner.
Lacy-winged dragonflies hovered
and darted over the water.

In the evening as the frogs sang their grumpy songs,
the deer came with their babies to drink
the water of the pond.
And black-masked raccoons prowled the water's edge
for tasty crayfish.

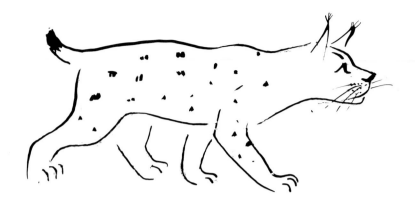

It didn't matter to the beavers who used their pond.
There was room for everyone, and the beavers
were too busy fixing the dam and repairing their houses
and raising their babies to notice their neighbors.
The paddling ducks, the sunning turtles,
and the slippery green frogs
sitting on lily pads meant nothing to them.
But while they worked, one old beaver
kept careful watch for the wolf.
He worried about the soft-footed lynx,
and his nose warned him of the stealthy wolverine.

With a *thwack* his tail slapped the water, and the beavers
dove for the shelter of their houses.
Then one by one their heads popped up.
Chirping and whistling they discussed the danger
that was past, and back to work they went.
While the beaver babies swam and splashed in
the limpid green light of their underwater world.

Then the late summer days felt the first nip of frost,
and the beavers were busier than ever, cutting down
more and more of the young aspens. They dragged
the branches into the water and buried them in the mud
at the bottom of the pond. The tender bark
would be their food through the bitter days of winter.

Now was the time for the ducks and blackbirds
to fly off to the southland.

The sumacs flamed scarlet, the aspens turned to gold.
And the frosted reeds rattled dryly in the cold wind.

The frost bit deeper and deeper into the ground
as a sheet of ice spread over the top of the pond.
And the frogs slept deep in the mud at the bottom.
The winter snows swept down, filling the hollows
and covering the secret runways of field mice.
The frozen earth slept under the snow.
The pond slept under the ice,
and the beavers were safe from the wolf,
the prowling lynx, and the wolverine,
under the icy roof of the pond and the frozen domes
of their houses.

But each spring the pond came back to life.
The melting winter snows and ice brought high water,
and the beavers worked frantically,
making their dam higher and stronger so that the water
wouldn't sweep it away.
And each spring there were more beaver families
with their babies, and new beaver houses.

The birds returned to build new nests.
The water quivered with young pollywogs and baby fish.
Again the mother deer picked their way
through the carpet of spring flowers
to bring their new fawns to drink.
But slowly, slowly, year by year,
things changed at the pond.
The ever-running stream
brought more than fish and water.
It carried with it fine dirt, which settled
on the bottom.
And little rivulets of muddy water
drained into the pond every time it rained.
As the years passed the pond grew smaller
and more shallow.
Little by little the reeds and cattails
along the shore moved out into the water.
At last the pond grew too small for all the beavers.
Farther and farther they had to roam from the safety
of the water in search of trees
to cut down for their food.

And the wolf, the lynx, and the wolverine grew bolder
as they crouched and waited for their prey.
So it was that in the early summer off went the beavers
down the stream
to find a new place for their home.
They left behind their long dam of sticks and mud,
and their empty beaver houses sitting in the water.
No longer did their chirps and whistles sound
across the pond.
No longer did the sharp slap of their tails
warn of danger.
And no longer were there bustling beavers
to repair the dam when the high spring water
flooded into the pond.

But the other small creatures still stayed.
The pond was big enough for frogs and fish.
The dragonflies still zoomed back and forth,
and the raccoons came cautiously at night,
looking for crayfish.
One early spring day, when all the snow
had melted suddenly,

a great flood of water came roaring down the stream
into the pond. Over the old dam it poured, and the rotted
sticks and branches could not hold the weight.

The torrent of water raced on down the brook,
and what was left of the pond went flowing out
through the break in the dam.

Once more the stream ran free.
Bit by bit the muddy floor of the old pond
turned green. Young plants sprang up
in the rich earth, and where once a pond
had caught and held the blue sky
there spread a green and grassy meadow
with a brook meandering through it.

But farther down, the beavers had already built
a new strong dam,
and a new pond sparkled in the sunlight.
Frogs and fishes, turtles and hovering dragonflies
enjoyed its waters.
Redwinged blackbirds nested in its rushes,
as ducks paraded their new babies proudly.
And in the cool evening light the mother deer
brought their young ones
to the edge of the pond to drink.

2 3 4 5 74 73 72